MLB's Greatest Teams

OAKLAND ATHLETICS

Big Buddy Books
An Imprint of Abdo Publishing
abdobooks.com

Dennis St. Sauver

abdobooks.com

Published by Abdo Publishing, a division of ABDO, PO Box 398166, Minneapolis, Minnesota 55439. Copyright © 2019 by Abdo Consulting Group, Inc. International copyrights reserved in all countries. No part of this book may be reproduced in any form without written permission from the publisher. Big Buddy Books™ is a trademark and logo of Abdo Publishing.

Printed in the United States of America, North Mankato, Minnesota.
102018
012019

 THIS BOOK CONTAINS RECYCLED MATERIALS

Cover Photo: Thearon W. Henderson/Getty Images.
Interior Photos: 33ft/Depositphoto (p. 7); AP Images (pp. 11, 17, 19, 23, 28); Christian Petersen/Getty Images (p. 25); Ezra Shaw/Getty Images (p. 9); FAY 2018/Alamy Stock Photo (p. 22); Jim McIsaac/Getty Images (p. 15); Justin Edmonds/Getty Images (p. 24); Paul Sakuma/AP Images (p. 13); PS/AP Images (p. 22); Ronald Martinez/Getty Images (pp. 24, 25); Rusty Kennedy/AP Images (p. 21); William Straeter/AP Images (p. 27); ZUMA Press, Inc./Alamy Stock Photo (pp. 5, 29).

Coordinating Series Editor: Tamara L. Britton
Contributing Series Editor: Jill M. Roesler
Graphic Design: Jenny Christensen, Cody Laberda

Library of Congress Control Number: 2018948450

Publisher's Cataloging-in-Publication Data

Names: St. Sauver, Dennis, author.
Title: Oakland Athletics / by Dennis St. Sauver.
Description: Minneapolis, Minnesota : Abdo Publishing, 2019 | Series: MLB's greatest teams set 2 | Includes online resources and index.
Identifiers: ISBN 9781532118128 (lib. bdg.) | ISBN 9781532171161 (ebook)
Subjects: LCSH: Oakland Athletics (Baseball team)--Juvenile literature. | Baseball teams--United States--History--Juvenile literature. | Major League Baseball (Organization)--Juvenile literature. | Baseball--Juvenile literature.
Classification: DDC 796.35764--dc23

Contents

Major League Baseball 4
A Winning Team 6
Oakland Coliseum 8
Then and Now 10
Highlights 14
Famous Managers 18
Star Players 22
Final Call 26
Through the Years 28
Glossary 30
Online Resources 31
Index 32

Major League Baseball

League Play

There are two leagues in MLB. They are the American League (AL) and the National League (NL). Each league has 15 teams and is split into three divisions. They are east, central, and west.

The Oakland Athletics is one of 30 Major League Baseball (MLB) teams. The team plays in the American League West **Division**.

Throughout the season, all MLB teams play 162 games. The season begins in April and can continue until November.

Stomper the elephant became the mascot for the Athletics in 1997.

A Winning Team

The Athletics team is from Oakland, California. The team's colors are green, gold, and white.

The team has had good seasons and bad. But time and again, the Athletics players have proven themselves. Let's see what makes the Athletics one of MLB's greatest teams!

Fast Facts

HOME FIELD: Oakland Coliseum

TEAM COLORS: Green, gold, and white

TEAM SONG: "They Are The Oakland A's" by Scott McCaughey

PENNANTS: 15

WORLD SERIES TITLES: 1910, 1911, 1913, 1929, 1930, 1972, 1973, 1974, 1989

Oakland Coliseum

The Athletics began playing in 1901 in Columbia Park Stadium in Philadelphia, Pennsylvania. The team moved two times before settling in the Oakland Coliseum in California in 1968.

The Coliseum has appeared in a couple of movies. In 1994, the movie *Angels in the Outfield* was filmed at the Coliseum. And in 2011, the movie *Moneyball* starring actor Brad Pitt took place there.

The Oakland Coliseum seats more than 47,000 baseball fans.

Then and Now

The Athletics began playing in Philadelphia in 1901. The team has been part of MLB for 117 years!

In the early years, the Athletics played in the World Series five times in ten years. The team led the league as players won three of those five Series.

Then from 1915 to 1921, the team placed last in its **division**. But shortly after, the Athletics won back-to-back World Series in 1929 and 1930.

Athletics fans lined the rooftops of homes outside the team's ballpark in Philadelphia. They all wanted to see the Athletics play the Chicago Cubs during the 1929 World Series.

Over the past 30 years, the Athletics players continued their success. The team played in five AL **Championships**, winning three of them. During that time, players won ten West **Division** titles.

The team also appeared in three more World Series games, winning once. In 1989, players beat the San Francisco Giants in four games.

> The Athletics were once called "White Elephants." That is because the club's symbol was an elephant standing on top of a ball.

Highlights

The Athletics team has been one of the best teams in all of baseball. It has won 15 AL **pennants**, 16 West **Division** titles, and nine World Series. From 1972 to 1974, the Athletics won three World Series titles in a row!

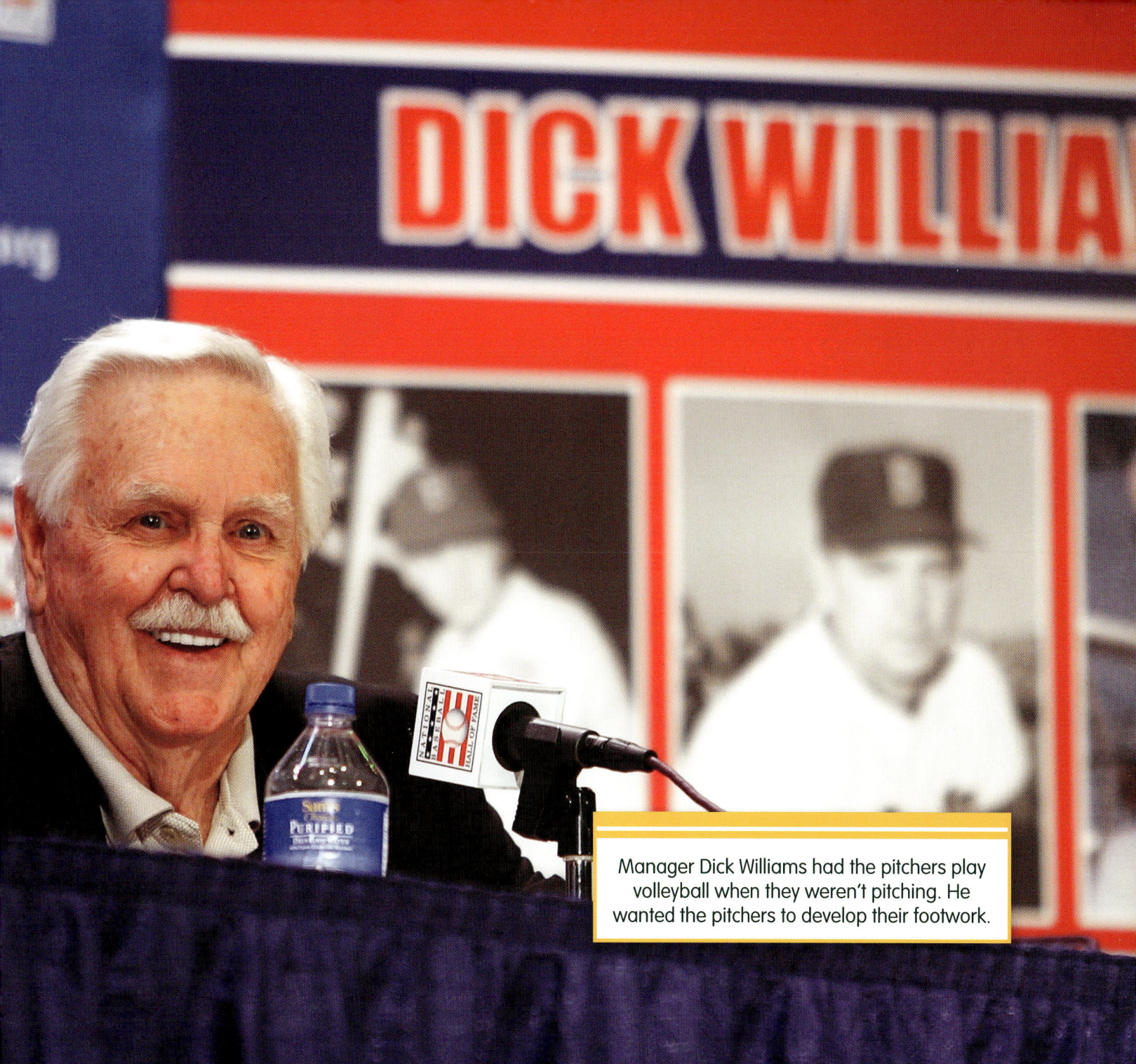

Manager Dick Williams had the pitchers play volleyball when they weren't pitching. He wanted the pitchers to develop their footwork.

In the 1980s, the Athletics continued to have great success. The team won two out of three AL **Championships**. Players beat the Boston Red Sox and the Toronto Blue Jays. But they lost to the New York Yankees.

In 1988, the team lost to the Los Angeles Dodgers in the World Series. But with good play the next year, the Athletics won it all in 1989! That year was the last time the Athletics took home a World Series title.

Win or Go Home

The top team from each AL and NL division goes to the playoffs. Each league also sends one wild-card team. One team from the AL and one from the NL will win the pennant. The two pennant winners then go to the World Series!

A team needs good players to win games. The Athletics traded star pitcher Vida Blue for seven players and money in 1978. The next year, the team lost 108 games.

Famous Managers

Connie Mack was the first manager of the Philadelphia Athletics. He continued coaching when the team moved to California. In total, he managed the Athletics team for 50 years!

Mack won 3,582 games as the team's manager. He also led the Athletics to five World Series wins. He was **inducted** into the National Baseball Hall of Fame in 1937.

Connie Mack's *(right)* career as player and manager outlasted eight US presidents! One of those presidents was Franklin D. Roosevelt *(left)*.

Tony La Russa began managing the Athletics in 1986. He led his team to three straight AL **Championships** from 1988 to 1990. In 1989, the team won the World Series.

La Russa won nearly 800 games in ten years with the Athletics. And the team won 19 **playoff** games under his leadership. La Russa earned four Manager of the Year Awards. He was **inducted** into the National Baseball Hall of Fame in 2014.

La Russa earned a law degree from Florida State University in 1978. But he chose baseball instead of law.

Star Players

Eddie Plank PITCHER

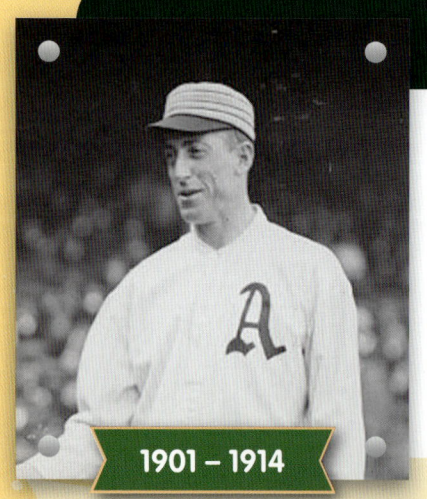

1901 – 1914

Eddie Plank was a pitcher during the team's early years. He was a three-time World Series winner in 1910, 1911, and 1913. He had eight seasons in which he won 20 or more games. Plank holds the MLB record for pitching 66 **shutouts** left-handed. He joined the National Baseball Hall of Fame in 1946.

Catfish Hunter PITCHER, #27

1965 – 1974

Catfish Hunter was an outstanding pitcher. He was selected for the AL All-Star team eight times. While with the team, Catfish pitched in three World Series. He won the Cy Young Award in 1974 for his talent on the mound. Catfish joined the National Baseball Hall of Fame in 1987.

Reggie Jackson OUTFIELDER, #9

Reggie Jackson was one of the best Athletics players. He played in 14 AL All-Star Games during his **career**. He was twice named **Most Valuable Player (MVP)** of the World Series. And in 1973, he was named the Major League Player of the Year. He hit 563 homers during his career. That is the fourteenth highest in MLB!

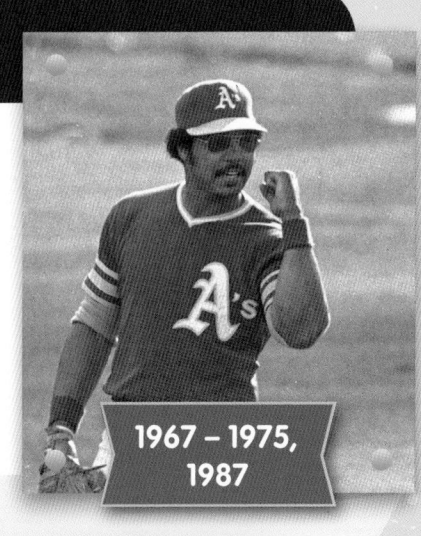

1967 – 1975, 1987

Rickey Henderson OUTFIELDER, #24

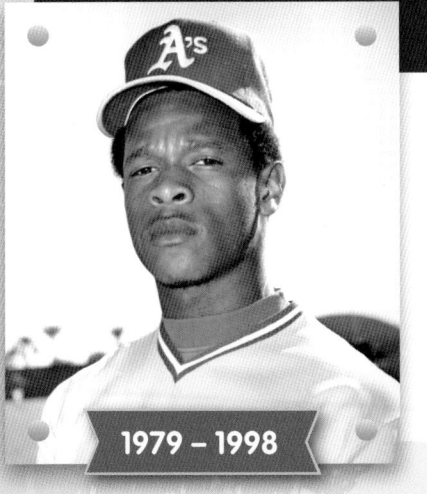

1979 – 1998

Rickey Henderson was nicknamed "Man of Steal." He was not Superman, but he was really fast! He had more than 100 **stolen bases** in three seasons. He was a ten-time AL All-Star and won three **Silver Sluggers**. Henderson earned the AL MVP Award in 1990.

Santiago Casilla PITCHER, #46

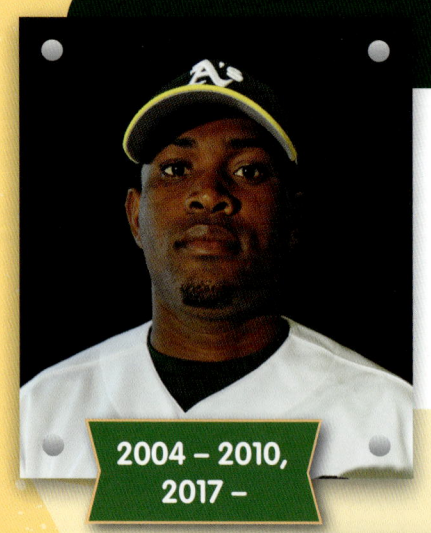

2004 – 2010, 2017 –

Santiago Casilla is from the Dominican Republic. He started playing for the Athletics in 2004 and was traded in 2010. Then, he came back to the Athletics in 2017. The team needed his talent and skill. Throughout his pitching **career**, Casilla has **struck out** nearly 500 batters.

Jed Lowrie SECOND BASEMAN, #8

Jed Lowrie is the starting second baseman for the Athletics. Lowrie continued his successful college career into the major leagues. He was a First Team **All-American** at Stanford University in 2004 and 2005. And he was picked in the first round of the MLB **draft** in 2005.

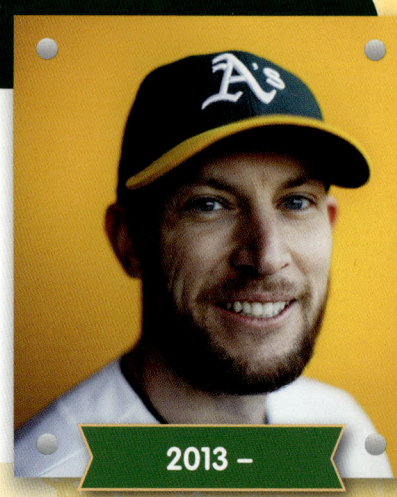

2013 –

Khris Davis LEFTFIELDER, #2

Khris Davis is a power batter. He joined the team in 2016. He has been a strong player ever since. In 2016, he hit 42 homers and 102 **runs batted in (RBIs)**. The next year, he hit 43 home runs and 110 RBIs. In 2017, Davis became the first Athletics player to hit 40 homers in back-to-back seasons.

2016 –

Jonathan Lucroy CATCHER, #21

2018 –

Jonathan Lucroy broke into the big leagues in 2010. He was traded to the Athletics in 2018. He was an All-Star team member in 2014 and 2016. And he was fourth in voting for NL **MVP** in 2014. Lucroy also earned the **Fielding Bible Award** for best catcher in 2014.

25

Final Call

The Athletics have a long, rich history. The team has played in 15 World Series, and earned nine World Series titles.

Even during losing seasons, true fans have stuck by the players. Many believe the Athletics will remain one of the greatest teams in MLB.

All-Stars

The best players from both leagues come together each year for the All-Star Game. This game does not count toward the regular season records. It is simply to celebrate the best players in MLB.

In 1965, owner Charles Finley brought a live mule to be the team's new mascot. The mule's name was Charlie O. He went everywhere with the team, including parties and games.

Through the Years

1905
The Athletics scored only three runs in five games of the team's first World Series.

1931
The Athletics won an outstanding 107 games!

1951
The team played its first night game at the Athletics' home field.

1960
Charles Finley became owner of the Athletics. He tried many new ideas for the team like using orange baseballs. He also offered money to players who could grow mustaches by Father's Day.

1970
Oakland used gold-colored bases at the team's home opener.

1988
The team won 14 games straight. That was the most back-to-back wins MLB had seen since 1977.

2018
Leftfielder Khris Davis led the league in home runs.

2012
Oakland won the AL West **Division** title for the fifth time in 13 years.

1992
Outfielder Rickey Henderson took his one-thousandth **stolen base** of his **career**.

Glossary

All-American selected as one of the best in the US in a particular sport.

career a period of time spent in a certain job.

championship a game, a match, or a race held to find a first-place winner.

division a number of teams grouped together in a sport for competitive purposes.

draft a system for professional sports teams to choose new players.

Fielding Bible Award an award given to the top defensive player at each position.

induct to officially introduce someone as a member.

Most Valuable Player (MVP) the player who contributes the most to his or her team's success.

pennant the prize that is awarded to the champions of the two MLB leagues each year.

playoffs a game or series of games to determine a championship or break a tie.

run batted in (RBI) a run that is scored as a result of a batter's hit, walk, or stolen base.

shutout a game or contest in which one side does not score.

Silver Slugger Award given every year to the best offensive players in MLB.

stolen base when a base runner safely advances to the next base, usually while the pitcher is pitching the ball to home plate.

strikeout an out in baseball that results from a batter getting three strikes during a turn at bat.

Online Resources

To learn more about the Oakland Athletics, visit abdobooklinks.com. These links are routinely monitored and updated to provide the most current information available.

Index

All-Star Game **23, 26**
All-Star team **22, 23, 25**
Angels in the Outfield (movie) **8**
awards **20, 22, 23, 25**
ballpark **6, 8, 9, 11, 28, 29**
Blue, Vida **17**
California **6, 18**
Casilla, Santiago **24**
Davis, Khris **25, 29**
division **4, 10, 12, 14, 16, 29**
Dominican Republic **24**
fans **9, 11, 26**
Finley, Charles **27, 28**
Henderson, Rickey **23, 29**
Hunter, Catfish **22**
Jackson, Reggie **23**
La Russa, Tony **20, 21**
league **4, 10, 12, 14, 16, 20, 22, 23, 25, 29**
Lowrie, Jed **24**
Lucroy, Jonathan **25**
Mack, Connie **18, 19**
mascot **5, 13, 27**
McCaughey, Scott **6**
Moneyball (movie) **8**
National Baseball Hall of Fame **18, 20, 22**
pennant **6, 14, 16, 23**
Pennsylvania **8, 11**
Pitt, Brad **8**
Plank, Eddie **22**
playoffs **16, 20**
Roosevelt, Franklin D. **19**
teams **8, 11, 12, 16, 18, 22, 25**
"They Are The Oakland A's" (song) **6**
Williams, Dick **15**
World Series **6, 10, 11, 12, 14, 16, 18, 20, 22, 23, 26, 28**